GLIMPSING GLORY

GLIMPSING GLORY

poems of
Living & Dying
Praying & Playing
Belonging & Longing

Catherine Lawton

CLADACH
Publishing

Glimpsing Glory

An AGATES Book of Poetry

Published by Cladach Publishing
Greeley, Colorado 80633
http://cladach.com

Cover art and Interior illustrations by Breanna Slike
ISBN-13: 9781945099151

To my father
George Herbert Cummings
1924-2019
a prophet of faith
a priest of mercy
a poet of love

"Hope"

LISTING
OF CONTENTS

REGARDING
THESE POEMS

What do I mean by 'glory'?

A taste, a flicker, a glimpse, a glimmer;
a flash, a whisper, a rustling breeze;
a fleeting moment that lingers on
taste buds, nerve ends, rides overtones of
sound, tingles with goose bumps of
closeness, surprise, recognition.

The Shekinah glory filled the temple.
Our bodies are temples.
Moses's face shone with the glory of
speaking face to face with God.
God is for us, with us, in us, among us;
but only in the glimpses—
usually coming uninvited, unexpected—
are we awake to God's presence
and life's mysteries and surprises.

We may be awakened in momentary,
sensory experiences—as the Spirit
hovers over our chaos—of beauty,
living things, a word spoken, thin places.

Glory is used to describe heaven,
or the 'other world'—another dimension,
perhaps a parallel world and existence.

The veil that separates the two seems
thick at times and thin at others.

It felt thick after my father died, and
in times of stress, worry, crisis
(until later, when I look back
and realize the 'voice' I heard,
the 'hand' that led, the 'way of escape'
that opened, were touches of glory in
the darkness, the hard places, the fog).

When I heard the stars sing, the veil was thin.

'From glory to glory'
(wrote Saint Paul),
or *'Gloire a gloire'*
(as I heard it preached in French).
'Glory!'
(as a child I heard the old saints exclaim).
*'If we don't praise him, the rocks are gonna
cry out, glory and honor!'*
(said an old spiritual sung in choir years ago).
'The Lamb who was slain is worthy to receive glory'
(heard John in his revelation vision).

> *'The glory and the freshness of a dream ...*
> *But yet I know, wher'ere I go,*
> *That there hath passed away a glory from the earth.*
> *...Where is it now, the glory and the dream?...*
> *Not in entire forgetfulness,*
> *And not in utter nakedness,*
> *But trailing clouds of glory do we come*
> *From God, who is our home...'* *
> (wrote Wordsworth, intimating immortality).

Perhaps the realm of glory isn't completely
different—or separate—from this one.
Perhaps all that is highest and best *here*—
good and true and beautiful—
is also found beyond the veil.
On this side, foretastes whet appetites,

clarify hopes, inspire visions,
create, and are created by, community.
Glory is where Eden, peace, wholeness,
light, fellowship, union dwell.

Glory is worth regarding slowly,
savoring and embracing savingly.

Moments when we experience glimpses
are worth holding, treasuring, sharing.

I.
Relating

SPACES BETWEEN

The spaces between things seem
to take on lives of their own.
Dark holes have shapes that move us.
Important nothings have megaphones.

A holding of breath between gusts,
hands so close don't quite touch,
a rest in a music score,
stillness before a storm.

Nothings open new possibilities
for something not yet that may be,
that heart place that nothing can fill
(or nothing has yet come to fit).

The dark shape watching me turns out
to be created by edges juxtaposed
of ferns, flowers, rocks, and shadows
(how fairies come to life, I suppose).

The spaces between things—between us—
compel, speak... entice....

SHIPS IN THE NIGHT

As loon's sweet sorrow slices fog,
I sail silently, saltily on currents,
your smile a wisp, an island in mists.

As keeling sprays and zephyr whispers,
your eyes deep, dark pools not fathomed:
Can one heart ever know another?

LOOK AT ME!

'Look at me, Cathy.'
Downcast, ashamed,
I shrank from seeing
my father's disappointment,
his sadness, maybe anger.

I was little; he was big.
I was guilty; he was right.
I was fearful; he was waiting.
I was stubborn; he persisted.

'Look at me, Cathy.'
The Father waits.
I avert my eyes,
not wanting to see
disappointment in His.

But He's persuasive,
and I'm learning
to turn,
to trust those eyes
of Love....

PROPHET-PRIEST PATERNAL

Gray eyes piercing
Deep voice convincing
Warm hands healing
  Fallow minds
  Fallen psyches
  Fellow souls

MAY-DAY BASKETS

Not as many May-first flowers here
   as in places I lived as a child—
where roses burst, clambered, climbed already,
     enough garden posies to revel in, make chains
     for garlands and necklaces, plenty to fill
     baskets for surprising the neighbors.
Now I could fill baskets with a few dandelion,
   chokecherry and crab apple blossoms.
Or I can let my cup overflow with gracious responses,
   pick loving words to give as lavish surprises.

CHILD IN ME

You waited while I caught up with you,
    child in me;
till I could see what you could see
    and set you free.

You waited with courage and watched with care
    all while I groped
to live my life in need of us
    but vague of hope.

Your impish ways allowed me glimpses,
    a coaster ride;
I caught a laugh, a cry, a sigh,
    but you played shy.

The saddened child would rise and I'd
    be sick and crying.
Not to be held or seen or heard,
    must feel like dying.

The needy child would seek attention
    and want some more
of what was offered to fill the void—
    a shifty shore.

The frozen child who couldn't move,
    by terror stricken,
had breathed the smoke and seen the flames
    that raged and licked.

The visioning child would dream of safe,
    delightful places,
to dance with elves and see the smiles
    in flower faces.

The playful child came out with puppies,
    a few friends and babies,
who didn't stay but opened windows
    on sunnier days.

The believing, trusting child heard the Word
    that rescued her.
She led the way for all the others
    needing Father/Mother.

I embrace you now; I see and hear
    and treasure you.
Let's hand-in-hand run free as one
    and live renewed.

'Unite my heart to revere your name,'*
    O, Lord, I pray.
And 'Lead us on a level path'**
    from day to day.

WATER UNDER THE BRIDGE

We were kids dropping
sticks off the bridge,
watching them splash,
catch in whirls,
tumble over rocks,
lodge in debris.
Some sailed smoothly
under and away, gone.
Others took time.

Time took us away
from that river bridge
to seas, coasts, plains
watered by other streams,
rooting in other shores;
till, years later, those
stuck sticks of dreamy
youth begin to dislodge
and float again, together—
worn, grayed, wiser—
on the relentless current
to the teeming ocean
where all streams lead.

WALK

Walk with me,
  not alone,
    along cool stream.
Rue the gloom,
  eschew doom.
The sky's above,
  the forest's green,
    heart's full of love.
Walk now,
  alone with me.

TOGETHER ON AN ISLAND

An island off the coast of Maine,
a dream, a celebration to anticipate,
has become a place where our feet
have felt: shell beaches and rocky
forest-floor trails, and lanes
rolling gently to shops of sundries,
coffee, muffins and crab rolls;
past Victorian New England cottages,
boat docks, lobster traps, and colorful,
multi-textured coastal gardens.

A house with rooms for us all;
harbors, salty breezes, gull calls;
wooded, quarry-cratered hills,
deep, rock-rimmed swimming holes
to jump in with flips and dives;
bicycles and scooters to ride,
kayaks to paddle the tides;
small boats and buoys in still...
soft ... sunset ... tableaus;
nature preserves with beaches
to comb for shells, skip rocks,
see Mew Gull, Osprey, Woodpecker,
Heron, Alder Flycatcher, Eider.

At table in the windowed porch,
we see a Deer step out of the woods.
One of us sights Jellyfish in high tide.
Another collects Sea Snails and so
is designated a 'traveling snailsman.'

A child exclaims at small Crabs,
green ones and spotted ones in tide pools.
A girl finds an elusive Sand Dollar,
a boy: smooth, translucent crescents,
a young man: Crab shells in shallows
and rocks skipping more than his fellows.

Locals and smiling vacationers,
bakers, artisans and shopkeepers,
fisherfolk and lobstermen enthuse,
'Be sure to swim in the quarry,
hike Tip Toe Mountain at dusk,
walk across the bridge to Lane Island,
visit the penny-candy counter—a must.
And come again!' ... I hope we can.

II.
Communing

BREATHING

Wind, not blowing,
entered my being
in a rain-soaked
old-growth
Redwood forest
as I inhaled sweetness
of damp sorrel,
dank ferns,
deep-needled floor,
and wisdom of
ancient trees,
their roots intertwined,
their heads drinking
coastal clouds,
as sun rays streamed,
sighed through fog
into that timeless
conscious moment.
Grounded.

THE STARS SING

Sleeping in a tent, we must take a walk
to the 'comfort station' in the night.
At 1:30—!—we pull out of sleeping bags,
put on shoes, take the dog for a hike.

Campfires and lanterns now out, we need
no flashlight in ethereal moonglow
bathing path, tents, boulders and pine trees,
peaks, and meadows below.

Fear of bears forgotten, I look up, away,
acquiesce to the serendipitous sight—
stars sprinkling the sky, a sparkling array
only imagined on lit suburban nights.

Like music engraved, blazoned across the sky,
notes—not in lined scores or measures,
but in splashes of compositions ears and eyes
aren't attuned to hear or decipher.

Not with physical ears do I hear the music
of stars singing out from night pavilion,
graced by the moon, echoed by bugling elk,
crooning owls and sibilant wind.

Celestial strains fill my soul with consolation,
comfort and swells of settled certainty
befitting constellations shining in place
since God sang the Heavens into being.

Nature sings back to God day and night,
I think, as we settle in our places—
born under stars, resting under starlight
listening to star-song cadences.

PIECES OF HEAVEN'S RADIANCE

White rocks glisten bright in gray gravel.
Flower petals catch sun, fade tomorrow.
Joyous waves splash, caress, then quail.
Stars pierce night, smile into sorrow.

Achingly beautiful glimmers,
foretastes call forth in me longing,
speak of what was and still lingers,
folding hope into strains of my song.

Seeing dimly through panes on this side,
we yearn, seek hints, strain for permanence.
Light shines through the pain in His side,
giving glints of the unseen till we dance
in Heaven's radiance.

SPRING TIME

Screen time
in spring
is deadening,
though perhaps
necessary.
But more needed
is the feel of
mountain breezes
in your lungs,
a rocky trail
under your feet,
the velvet of
unfurling leaves,
sweet scents of
new-mown grass
and just-turned earth,
the taste of
first strawberries.

BACKYARD IN SPRING

I look across the grassy yard
   and what do I see?—
big, round bunny eyes
   gazing back at me.

Then a flash of furry tail—
   squirrel up a tree;
he flicks his tantalizing flag
   and scolds down at me.

I see a lumpy creature hop
   under beans and beets—
croaking out his private joy
   in garden damp and sweet.

Feathery friends in flowery shrubs,
   harmonic bird song—
in our backyard refuge calling
   forth the day long.

SPRINGTIME REUNIONS

Welcome back, friends, I'm bringing you seeds,
  birds in the bushes, birds in the trees.
Call and chatter, whistle and cheep,
  birds on the grasses, birds on the breeze.

Display your colors, showcase your tune;
  she'll hear, she'll see you—she's coming soon.
Sing from the housetop, she's perched at the gate;
  who could resist such a spirited mate?

Birds playing games of 'catch me if you can,'
  soon build their nests in Hawthorn and Linden.
Eggs warm, babies fed, they fledge and remember;
  next spring to show up, back at my feeder.

GRACKLE JAZZ BAND

A ways along my path, it was toward end of day,
  a spring attraction broke into my reverie.
A band of Grackles perched atop a Locust stage,
  all seven bards a-swayin' top the ragged tree.

The jammin' Grackles, oh my, what a sound they made
  with voices mixing in a grand improvisation.
This concert was no sweetly-singing serenade,
  but syncopated, animated harmonization.

A bossy bass was unrestrained with tempo shifts.
  The stringy strummers threw in chords of dissonance.
As soulful pickers played along with fitful riffs,
  the brash blues singers crooned a song with confidence.

Their ballad was cacophonous to celebrate
  the migrant destinations and the spring love pledged,
of groovin' moves they made to win their feathered mates;
  of feeders, hawks and foxes, and of young birds fledged.

With polyphonic sound above the competition
  of Robins' chirp and Finches' flute and Red-wings' yodel,
the raucous Grackle jammers held my rapt attention,
  until their session faded ... into ... shade and shadow.

IN NATURE

There I have recognized
Experienced
The presence of God
Present to, for, with, among, through
What God made and loves:
Seashore and mountains, desert and plains
Farm fields, vineyards and orchards
Rocks, trees, leaves, and flowers
Birds
Creeks
Croaking frogs
Puddles with mirror effect
Floating worms and leaves
Fish and wildlife
Salty ocean
Cool mountain breezes
Rain on native summer grasses
Shadows/clouds/mirages/rainbows/reflections
Moon, stars, sky
Morning dew
Golden evening light
Mosses, lichens, decomposing logs
Forest floors
Nature's gardens

WHAT IS COMING TO OUR WORLD?
How a Backyard Bird Sees Christmas*

Seasons have passed of warm, wiggly worms,
bountiful gardens and bright wildflowers,
plentiful insects on leaf and wing,
sun traveling high across the sky,
and all good things that make us sing.
The days grow shorter. The air grows colder.
We search now for meals and warm roost.
When the hawk and fox come hunting,
I will quickly hide in a bush.
The chill in the air tells me high on the peaks
snowflakes are drifting in piles white and deep;
soon, in this place that's home to me
frost will sparkle and snow will fall.
Creator God, who gives sunshine and seeds,
berries and water, spring, summer, fall—
surely wants us to thrive all year long!

Bells are ringing. I hear singing.
Good aromas are increasing.
What should we anticipate?
What story does the music relate?
When the people open their doors,
I smell something warm, spicy and sweet,
and the seeds they bring to us are nice.
Nippier days turn their noses pink,
but something good is coming, I think.
Anticipation fills the air.

Nights are cold, but lights are bright
and they twinkle everywhere.
It looks like stars are coming down
on trees and houses from the air.

It looks to me—all around—
like Heaven's surely coming down!

Children come bounding out in the snow,
all rosie and bundled for winter play.
They gather greenery, seedpods, and cones—
much like we do sometimes in spring.
I wonder what they're going to make?
A blue-eyed girl and boy look my way.

I start to fly; then I hear the girl say,
'Hello, little bird. Here's a present for you.
Do you know that tomorrow is Christmas Day?'
The boy says, 'Merry Christmas to you, little bird,
and happy celebrations with your friends, too.'
I like the peanut butter and seeds they've pressed
into the pine cones they hang in the tree.

I'll fly to the highest branch and sing
a song of Heaven coming down,
light in the darkness, warmth in the cold,
provision and plenty, promises of old.
As seeds wait patiently within the earth,
there's hope for us all—even little birds.
All feathered friends, all four-legged creatures,
all living things, now hear my song.
All who Creator God called 'good':
God cares—and comes—for all.

I will sing the song God gives me.
I will wing the flight that lifts me.
I will listen to the glorious sounds,
for Heaven's love is all around.

Christmas has come!

BUSHTITS

Sprite and nimble on honeysuckle:
   tiny, frisky,
   little flock
   hopping and feeding on
   sprigging branches—

Tink, tink, tinkling like bells that ding
   each way they turn;
   hopping over,
   around, between, and
   upside downing.

Buffy breasts, sporting gray
   on back and wings;
   bluffy faces,
   longish tails and
   puff-ball bodies—

Bringing ringing into my morning.

MOUNTAIN BLUEBIRDS

Leaving the hillside trail that wends
   upward, midst rocks and trees,
   I step
   onto meadow of sunshine and breeze.

Startling
   a flock of mountain birds that
   lift out of spring-blooming grasses
   in breath-taking blueness
   of wing and breast
   imbued with hues that capture
   sky and lake and hints of wildflower.

They infuse and tint my imagination
   with a shade
   by which to measure
   every blue
   thereafter.

NATURE DOESN'T LIE*

Nature's truth presents in facets, angles
    of perspective,
    changing light,
    filtering seasons.
Observe in stages or you won't know its truth,
    not with
    one camera click
    or drive-by look.
It doesn't show you its whole self all at once;
    be still,
    listen,
    feel.
Recognition, Respect, Revealing come
    in mutuality.
    Knowing
    happens there.
Be present to a flower, tree, or pond;
    it will gradually
    be present
    to you in truth.

BLOOD AND DUST

We forget who we are and whose,
fragmented within and from, lost
in a fog of blurs and gaps, with so
many trajectories and so many
windows competing on a screen.

But because God born human
breathed the earthy air we breathe,
walked on dirt with tender feet,
loved his friends with beating heart,
saw creation with lidded eyes,
spoke with tongue and lips to all he
spoke into being at the beginning;

Because Jesus' human, God-infused
blood dropped into our dust of being,
windows can integrate, open to where
what is meant, intended, and spoken,
coalesces now and newly into Life.

III.
Trusting

48

A SINFUL WOMAN WHO LOVED MUCH
(in Luke 7:36-50)

My tears made mud on his dusty feet.
  My hair caked with dirt paths he trod.
My sighs rode the wind of the air he breathed.
  My hands touched the face of God.*

His eyes entered mine to unlock my grave.
  His feet didn't shrink from my touch.
He smiled like a child,** held the love I gave.
  How could he forgive so much?!

FLUNG TO THE STARS

Nothing is wasted,
nothing is lost,
nothing can doom us,
nothing needs corrupt—
only be tossed.

So...

Standing, I fling my
burdens to the sky. They
fly into stars that flare
brighter and hotter,
rhapsodizing a story
of rest and release;
glory, all glory
to God the Father.

TAKE AND EAT

The preacher stands and breaks fresh bread
   then pours the cup with liquid red.
But some folks' jaws are clenched so tight,
   they cannot chew a heartening bite.

And some whose eyes are glued on others,
   they miss the free and sumptuous offer.
Some deaf from dark, incessant lies,
   will hear no call to 'Come and dine.'

And some, whose festering wounds disable,
   they cannot find their place at table.
As he holds life, expresses thanks—
   the priest will listen for an echoing 'Yes.'

But are the bitter mouths now pursing,
   accustomed more to gripes and cursing?
Do pointing fingers form tight fists
   that can't acknowledge gracious gifts?

And will the deceived and bound give praise,
   let life and truth break free of chains?
Will all the lame and feeble kneel
   to catch the crumbs and drops that heal?

The bread and wine, though broken and blessed,
   each one must take, receive;
   each one must freely ingest.

OUT OF THE HEART

If the central room of a house
   echoes with laughter, prayer, and music,
   then love works out through peripheral rooms
   to bring order to seeming chaos,
   let light into hidden places,
   allow fresh breezes into stuffy spaces,
   reveal ways forward out of cluttered halls
   to welcome others in.

Out of the heart the mouth speaks.
Out of the heart the arms reach.
Out of the heart the feet step.

Does the mouth speak truth in love?
Do the arms reach to give consolation?
Do the feet step gladly to serve?

When inner rooms lie dank, unused,
   furniture with dust effaced,
   walls with spider webs laced,
   light bulbs never replaced;
   not reaching, but peeking through cracks,
   false fronts, boarded windows, locked doors;
   not speaking, but pursed like a bat in rafters.
   Then the mouth croaks as a hostage
   creeping like roach in the dark;
   forgetting the home's real heart,
   forgetting the heart's true home,
   unable to open to light and breath.

LOVE'S ENTICEMENT

Only the One Who made us
    and that for which we are made
    will entice us, finally.
When we learn what glitters isn't gold,
when we listen to the song we thought too old,
    we'll turn and see love's purity.

NOTHING TOO HARD

No rock too hard for your love
    to suffer
    to rescue
    to heal.
If your always-present wooing
meets responses you're pursuing:
    the 'yes'
    of listening
      co-operating
      co-creating,
thy will will be being done,
which is to enfold in radiant wings,
    enter our pain
    soften our flint
    re-direct our fight
    squeeze good surprises
      out of bad plights.

PURPOSE

We live in this in-between time,
by faith,
and by Jesus' Spirit
to live in and show
the good
the fellowship
the victory
the mercy
the beauty of
God of Love
to all people—and to all creation.

We live here to worship and praise
by faith
from our hearts
our Creator
God
of love
of truth
of presence
of goodness
of hope
for each of us—and for all creation.

IN THE MORNING

Rain falls.
Dust settles.
Light dawns.
Mercy comes.

WHEN MOTHER SANG

I heard mystery and longing,
I heard certitude of things unseen,
I heard an earthy person give voice
to an other-worldly something.

Especially when she shared her story
of being an orphan, forsaken—yet not;
of being adopted, accepted, rescued;
given a name, a family, a home.

When Mother sang, I heard sadness
and joy intermixed, as in this life
we long for something lost and for
something sure—but not yet.

ALPHA AND OMEGA

Did God put us in this time bubble
   to distantly observe our troubles—
   a grand Experiment?

Or does God create, love, experience
   with, in time, necessarily—
   a grand Fulfillment?

And is that love creating, self-giving
   ever freely, perseveringly—
   a grand At-one-ment?

Are we destined to live or die with—
   or without—the just God—
   a grand Arbitration?

Or are we made of God stuff that
   will return, respond to, rest in
   the grand Romancer?

Either way, surely, all begins and ends
in the mind and heart of God.

WAYSIDE

Off every pleasant way are
waste places, unforged, where
herbs grow wild demeanors
and a ditch is a deep gorge.

I've heard of wayfarin' strangers
in a song of wistful lay;
but 'poor and plaintive souls'?:
Heirs of love are called to hope.

When clouds are dark, waygoing late,
then love may lead by thorny paths,
but taking the hand, the next step—
leads to a bright and wider land.

IV.
LIVING

LOOSE ENDS

At pieces jettisoned in change and hurry
I now strain to grasp, at dismembered pictures
swirling here and there in fog and flurry;
catch a glimpse, a tease, a hint, a blur.

Unfinished business, unaccomplished dreams,
unrequited longing, unacknowledged gaze,
uncompleted circles and unchained links,
loose ends flapping in memory's breeze.

Too many partings, too many doors
closed without touch or intent or goodbye;
too many words left unsaid, unmoored;
too many words left said, there lie.

I WAS YOUNG, NOW I AM...?

I thought I had something to say, but
  people thought I was younger than I was;
    I wanted to be a teenager so they
    wouldn't think I was *just* a child.
  I wanted to be a young adult so
    they wouldn't consider me *just* a teenager
    (but I'd surely never age over thirty!).
  Then finding myself thirty,
    I wanted to be in middle age, so
    they wouldn't think me too young to speak,
    with nothing to say.

But I was still a 'Baby Boomer,'
  a generation who thought
  we'd never grow old.
But how old is old?
  Am I there yet?—Maybe so.
  Will 'they' listen now?
  Have 'they' heard at all?

Inside I'm still the child, the teen,
  the young adult, the mid-lifer, and
  finding myself ... where? ... here?
Now what?—
  Go back to the past that I
    never fully appreciated?
  Park in the present and refuse to move farther?
  Re-focus and set my sights on the stars,
    let the wind fill my sails and take me ...
    where?

FLOATING

Floating like a cloud, I lift
  above dead weights
  and throbbing fears.

Glowering clouds hang down,
  drop hard in pools
  of anguished tears.

Clouds won't sail without a wind;
  I risk unmooring
  and escape—soaring.

Birds-eye views reveal below
  the shadows cast
  by clouds that float.

IF WE HAD KNOWN, WOULD WE HAVE BEGUN?

We felt so ready
so wise
(in our own eyes).
We knew enough;
but how little that was.

Still, slow and steady,
trial and error,
(I'm looking in the mirror),
the path comes rough.
When will we have learned?

HIGH SCHOOL CLASS REUNION

Returning to that place where
 fog-swirled distance and time
 obscure faces and figures,
 cloud memories with passing
 years of changing sands and
 irrepressible tides and waves
 crashing against my shore.

Like hoary forests in the mist,
 so distant are the faces,
 so vague my place among them.
Then, drawing closer, I perceive
 one tree, then two, then three
 faces, eyes, an expression
 I saw daily those four years.

Then voices, then names;
 and they look back at me;
 and as recognition dawns
I see a dormant, long-neglected,
 almost forgotten part of myself.
 My life has moved on:
 Did I think theirs hadn't?

I reach out a hand and discover
 nothing is lost, only seasons
 have passed—fresh spring
 and long, fruitful summer—
But so much gained in autumn,
 finding myself on mutual ground,
 still rooted and remembered.

CONTRAST

Unlike dreams crowded with
   vague faces, dim figures
   and indecipherable
   expectations,
Clear-eyed memories live:
   shared moments
   light with laughter,
   unfiltered exuberance.
Once we lay in a pickup
   riding home after
   running in sand,
   splashing in waves,
Singing silly songs,
   counting stars appearing;
   no demands or
   cloudy contingencies;
Unwary of yesterday, tomorrow,
   but open-hearted ...
   being ... here ...
   free.

GIVE ME A MAN

Give me a man with hair on his arms
who smells of honest work (but not too long);
who knows how to shoot, cast a line,
hammer a nail and plant a pine.

Give me a man with a creased leather Bible
who can lead in prayer (but not too long);
who sings in both melody and harmony
songs of faith and love and family.

Give me a man who knows how to laugh
and how to cry with me (but not too long);
who'll take my hand, lift my sights above,
and show—not just tell—that he loves.

Give me a man who makes and not breaks,
who works before he plays (but not too long);
who builds and repairs and binds up
the places that lay gashed and corrupt.

Give me a man who guards the edges
of togetherness (but not too much);
who protects—not contains—my heart
when we're together and when apart.

Now that's a man to cherish through life,
to walk with (as long as life lets you);
no matter what comes, you can stand—
with a man who is really a man.

COURAGE!

Scottish forebears wore it as rampant lion
     on their crest.
Presbyterian forebears received it as gracious,
     sovereign gift.
Methodist forebears found it in holy love and
     consecration.
Revolutionary forebears took it, valiant for
     honor and right.
It rose in the hearts of foremothers, steadfast
     at hearth.
Through all these, though struggling to make
     it mine,
I've been fortified.

GLORY—

'To the newborn king,'
   let angel voices ring.

'Glory,' saints would shout;
but now rocks cry out.
   'Glory and honor.
      Ain't got time to die.'

Glory sacrifices praise,
hides in the child's lay,
   'Back of the clouds,
      the sun is always shining.'

None is worthy to express
the glory of Heaven's best;
   but One revealed in Shekinah
   will have glory and honor.

So rise, shine, and give it!

V.
DYING

GOD'S ECOLOGY

Unless the bloom of this
    season dies,
Spring's new possibilities
    can't arise.

THE WAKE

(After a Cottontail bunny fell into—and
died in—a basement window well)

The fly circles,
  buzzing a dirge over
  the still-fluffy fur,
  the still form stiffening.
The father toad,
  eyes closed as if
  in prayer, stays close,
  attends.

FORGET-ME-NOTS

If you remember me,
don't let your remembrance be
of complaining or whining or
fierce defense of the right.
Let these fade as the flowers.

And if the stems of good deeds,
encouraging words, shared thoughts
are too slim to stick in the ground
of memory, let them die too.

But know: some impulse for good
lives in the Soil, feeds our roots,
creates new shoots
out of death and decay.

Yes, remember this:
that hope and love and beauty,
though dimly seen here, abide,
hold seeds of a future Garden
that forgets you not.

SO CLOSE BUT SO FAR

Death, be not proud nor
cast shadowy tentacle
like vise round my heart.
This parting is temporal.

Boulders rolled like pebbles;
veil tore like gauze; now
with inner light we gaze.
To inner voice we listen.

BEDSIDE VIGILS

BESIDE THE CRIB OF MY NEWBORN

Freshly arrived from Heaven's glory,
    trailing shiny clouds.
I stroke the peachy cheek.
Eyelids flutter as if knowing angels.
Each infant grin received as smiling
    gladness of life.
Dreams alight;
    I wonder who and what you'll be.

BESIDE THE DEATHBED OF MY FATHER

Prolonged departure to Heaven's glory,
    gathering shiny clouds.
I stroke the pale cheek.
Eyelids flutter as if greeting angels.
Each fading grin taken as acceptance
    of soon release.
Memories abide;
    I cherish who and what you've been.

But what will you be?

LET IT GO
(Death to Self)

In times when darkness
threatens and I begin
to feel the leers and aches
of slights and innuendos again;

As light dims and night rims
round my free vision,
Mother Jeanne comes to me
with words of wisdom:

'Let it go.'

'It doesn't go easy. It hurts.'
'Yes; but to hold gives it power,
to speak and repeat gives credence.
Release—the air will clear.'

I let it go—

by opening—as she taught—
curtains wide for sunshine,
looking out through windows bright.
And love wins another time.

WHEN I LIE DYING

Don't pretend all is fine—death's our enemy.
    But take my hand, save tears for the morrow.
Trust together—this darkness is conquered.
    Know all will be well; plan to follow.

Be there, if you can, but don't hold me;
    release—as I must do, too.
Till your time will come to cross over
    entrust me to Love, as I you.

Persevere—only shadows, misty veils
    divide these two blessed places.
Climb the mounts, cross the seas, walk the valleys
    till again I will see your dear faces.

QUESTIONS OF LIFE AND DEATH

Bodies house spirits
which shine through eyes,
speak through a voice,
serve, construct, lift
through hands.

His body died, but
his spirit lives—has
away, escaped, gone.
Then tell me, does the
give-and-take live on?

What his eyes gave
I carry still, but when
I'm gone, who will? Are
memories dead in his brain
or spirit-retained?

Words he spoke emanate,
lodging in one, shared
with another. Sounds
will travel toward star dust
as ashes to earth.

His work, healing touch
is built on and growing
through others' hands,
though earthly dwellings
are long demolished.

We've taken of his essence.
Whence, whither his spirit?
Does it carry his DNA code?
Surely the language of God,*
once spoken, lives on.

HERE TO ETERNITY

He has left this world of time
   and entered eternity?
But we aren't, all, there yet.

The fullness of time will come?
   Meanwhile we wait
and yearn for completion.

Are they waiting, watching,
   somehow incomplete in
realms of fulfillment and rest?

Are we caught now in a time
   bubble destined to pop
and release, reunite, expand?

But this moment holds all eternity
   like a drop of the ocean.
Eternal waters feed, carry moments.

VI.
PRAYING

WORTHY TO RECEIVE GLORY

Made to honor, we give fealty.
We seek true north like a needle.
But to look for your king
   in a pulpit, disappoints;
   in a government, fails;
   in the mirror, distorts.
Look instead with the eyes of your heart
   to the Wounded who heals;
   to the Throne that is true;
   to the Lamb who was slain,*
      Christ the King.

A PRAYER

Let Your sweetness sweeten me.
Let Your light illumine me.
Let the darkness flee from me.
As I rest in Thee.

PRAISE THE RISEN ONE IN DEED!

As God's own
dear ones,
created out of love
in the first place,
to whom he showed
a Face
and joined with
forever
in the God-man,
living and dying for,
being ever present to,
influencing for good
always;
We have more help—
and hope—
than we begin
to conceive.
We have more reasons
to celebrate
than we begin
to believe.
But let us begin—
Let us praise God
in deed.

WE DON'T KNOW HOW TO PRAY AS WE OUGHT

If I say 'please,'
    will my waiting heavenly Father give what I ask?
If we all hold hands in a circle,
    will others' faith make up for my lack?
Will it help if I tell God
    every minute detail of what I need and want?
Will adding the words 'In Jesus' name'
    make Sovereign God less resistant?
If we pray on our knees,
    will the Almighty see and honor our humility?
If we acknowledge God's feminine side,
    will Our Mother have mercy?
If we pray in angelic languages,
    will the Spirit understand us better?
Will loud and preacherly, or whispered prayers,
    bend God's ear closer?
Will candles or incense lift the sense
    of my prayers to God's holy nostrils?
Will my tears of regret, sorrow and repentance
    make God's heart thrill?
If we listen long enough to find and pray God's will,
    will it have to be done?
If I breathe my devotion all day long,
    will I be favored to approach God's throne?

Yes ... maybe ... and no.

Does the Spirit, Who searches hearts intimately
    and knows the mysterious
mind of the Father,
    intercede for us in groanings

both kind and efficacious,
all because of Jesus' self-giving,
others-empowering love* most gracious?

Can my will be transformed by God's will,
   my hands and feet join God's actions,
   my heart be energized by Father's love,
   my desires unite with Spirit's intercessions,
   my labors yoke with Jesus' work,
   and my prayers find fruition in co-creation?

Yes ... yes ... and yes!

LOVE SONG OF THE KING

The Singer sings because he is Song;
the Lover loves because he is Love;
the Maker creates because he is Creativity;
the King rules because he is Sovereign.

The song resounds in nature's cadences;
the love abounds in magnetic call;
the creativity resurrects from every death;
the order rearranges chaotic depths.

Sing over this dust, O Word of Life,
love incomprehensible, yet mine;
create of this clay newness to rise
infused with the song of the King.

SEEING THROUGH A GLASS

Like Cosmo* in MacDonald's story within a story,
    we see through a glass, not yet face to face.
We welcome the spirit of our desired one
    into our lodgings, our sanctuary, our heart.
We seek to remove what grieves the one—
    things of death; instead, bring in beauty and life.
We adore the one whose reflection we see,
    want to please, content to gaze on such beauty,
perfection, faithfulness … even unto revealing of
    suffering love.

WHOLENESS AND PEACE

Lord, I don't want to live out of
a place formed by other people's
brokenness, false words spoken
over me, lies internalized, nor fears.

I don't want others' pain, wounds,
fears, let alone my own, to
determine my responses, choices,
to be my truth, urge my actions.

Speak Truth in this awakened place.
I open doors, windows, pull down
storm shutters, even plank by plank,
that your Light may stream in.

Help me take the child by the hand,
hold her, try to understand and
open eyes and heart to listen,
to hear what's being given.

Help me give up the need for answers,
find wholeness, peace in surrender.

A MORE EXCELLENT WAY?

When I was a child, I
prayed like a child
to God above,
folding hands
closing eyes
repeating words
talking to Jesus.
Not knowing
the soft wind
whispering,
branches lifting
were also prayer.
When I learned
to listen with
Spirit-pierced ear
my prayers became
shorter but more
continuous.
Recently,
the gaze—
eye to eye
heart to heart—
blends praise
confession
lamentation
supplication
waiting
knowing
resting
in One.

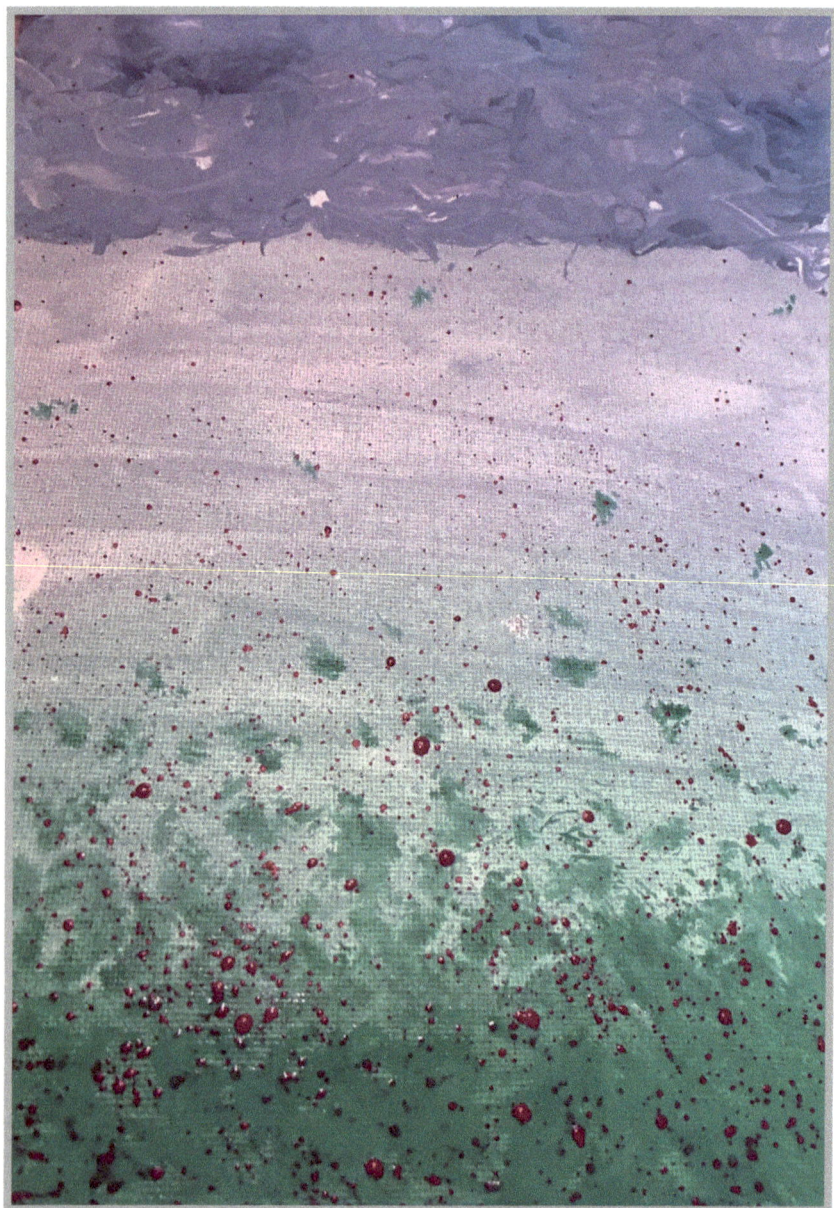

VII.
WORD-PLAYING

A MIGHTY POEM

"Mighty my liking for this beverage—guess which?"

"Might 'T' be the letter with which it begins?"

"My Tea, oh yes! I'll take some now, if you please."

"Might 'e like some too?—and might she?"

TO DUST OR NOT TO DUST?

Dust I must;
no choice, it seems.
Dust is showing
in the sun beams.

Leave it there?
or clear the air?

It makes a soft
patina, right?
We can always
dim the lights.

CANINE SOCIAL MEDIA

My dog, Jasper, reads
  pee mail with his nose.
And he's a dexterous texter
  as he lifts four toes.

Some moms dole out tech time;
  but me? I give trek time.
Each bush, post, and bench
  offers doggy wi-fi.

When he wiggles and whines
  and starts to holler,
I lace up my shoes, click
  the links of his collar.

When he meets other dogs, it's
  'Will you be my friend?
Follow me in the net-erhood,
  my hashtag's a trend.'

Dogs carry screen names
  on their behinds;
Cuz that's where they sniff,
  their profiles to find.

With his nose he scans lawns
  for the latest chatter
from cute Lily on the corner
  or Bruce the Irish Setter.

COULDA, SHOULDA, WOULDA

(Three Scenarios)

1.

Wouldja've done it
if you coulda
or if they paidja
enough?
Wouldja sell your soul
that way?

2.

If you coulda done it,
wouldja've?—even
if some judged ya
or begrudged ya?
Or wouldja hide your light
away?

3.

If you coulda and you knew
that you shoulda
but you didn't
do that thing,
wouldja ask forgiveness when
you pray?

God loves ya, all the same!

BRECCIATED

We're badly skewed,
  in hard cohesion,
  trying to get our due.
Our indurated hearts test
  flinty, steely,
  ossified, crusted
  and seared.
But earthquakes happen,
  faults shake
  and epic floods
  shift, carve,
  break, crack, fill.
Veins of flow form gemstones
  infused with
  crystal inclusions.

A PREPOSITIONAL PROPOSITION

Does God come *at* us? Or *to* us?
Is Jesus' eye angry *at*? Or sad *for,
with, by, alongside*? Joyful *over,
because of*? Or loving *toward*?

Does God come *at* us to judge,
condemn, punish, or shame?
Or come *to* us *out of* love, *under-*
girding, lifting *up*, rescuing *from*?

You might feel God comes *at* you—
like a cloud *upon*, a force *around*,
a persuasion *over*, attraction *toward*
that seems irresistible *within, without.*

But acting *at* is control *from above.*
Acting *to, with, for*—self-giving love.

Why resist?

HOLEY

What
gets bigger
the more you
take away from it?
'A hole' says the pun.
'I don't know' says one
shocked by shovels
jaded by spades
pricked by picks
cut, pierced
scraped, scooped
turned and tamped.
Then as water pours in,
the enlarged heart
has purpose
fullness
life.

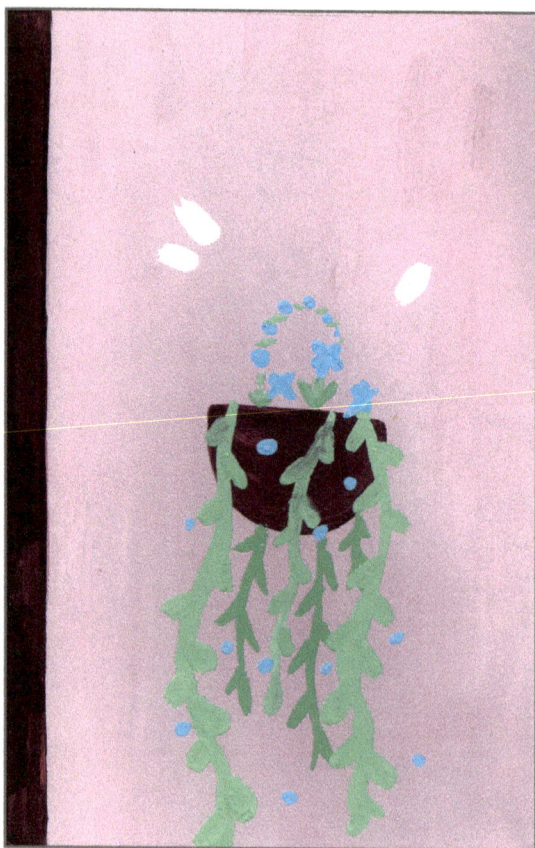

NOTING
SOURCES AND INFLUENCES

NOTES ON THE INTRODUCTION:

pp. 11-13: Representative Scriptures alluded to: Exodus 34:29 and 40:34; Psalm 19:1; Luke 19:40; 1 Corinthians 3:16; 2 Corinthians 3:7, 18; Colossians 1:15-17; 1 Timothy 3:16; Revelation: 5:12

p. 12: Lines quoted from the poem, "Ode: Intimations of Immortality from Recollections of Early Childhood" by William Wordsworth (first published 1807).

NOTES ON INDIVIDUAL POEMS:

p. 22-23: "Child in Me"
    Scriptures referenced: *Psalm 86:11 **Psalm 143:10 (NRSV)
    This poem, and "Floating" on p. 65, inspired by Janyne McConnaughey's story in her memoir, *BRAVE: A Personal Story of Healing Childhood Trauma* (Cladach, 2018).

pp. 40-41: "What Is Coming to Our World?"
    Originally written for the Lawton's grandchildren, and later published as a story-in-verse picture book by the same title (Cladach, 2018); here slightly edited.

p. 44: "Nature Doesn't Lie"
    Written after viewing an exhibition of paintings by Claude Monet, entitled "The Truth of Nature," at the Denver Art Museum; and after reading Richard Rohr's Daily Meditation series, "Science: Old and New" and "Art: Old and New."

p. 49: "A Sinful Woman Who Loved Much"
    Inspired by meditating on the story in Luke 7:36-50.
    Christians believe *Jesus Is the 'face of God' given to humankind, making God personal, approachable, and knowable for each of us, and that Jesus is the **Child (Son) of God, innocent, pure, and trusting of the Father.

p. 82: "Questions of Life and Death"
    *Line 28 taken from the title of the influential book, *The Language of God* by Francis Collins (Free Press, 2006).

p. 87: "Worthy to Receive Glory"
    *Inspired by listening, as if for the first time, to a reading of Revelation 5, especially verses 6 and 12.

p. 90-91: "We Don't Know How to Pray as We Ought"
    * "Self-giving, others-empowering love" is how Thomas Jay Oord defines God's nature in his influential book, *The Uncontrolling Love of God* (IVP Academic, 2015).

p. 93: "Seeing through a Glass"
    *Cosmo is the main character in a story within a story, *Tale of Cosmo*, in George MacDonald's *Phantastes: A Faerie Romance for Men and Women* (first published 1857, available in many editions).

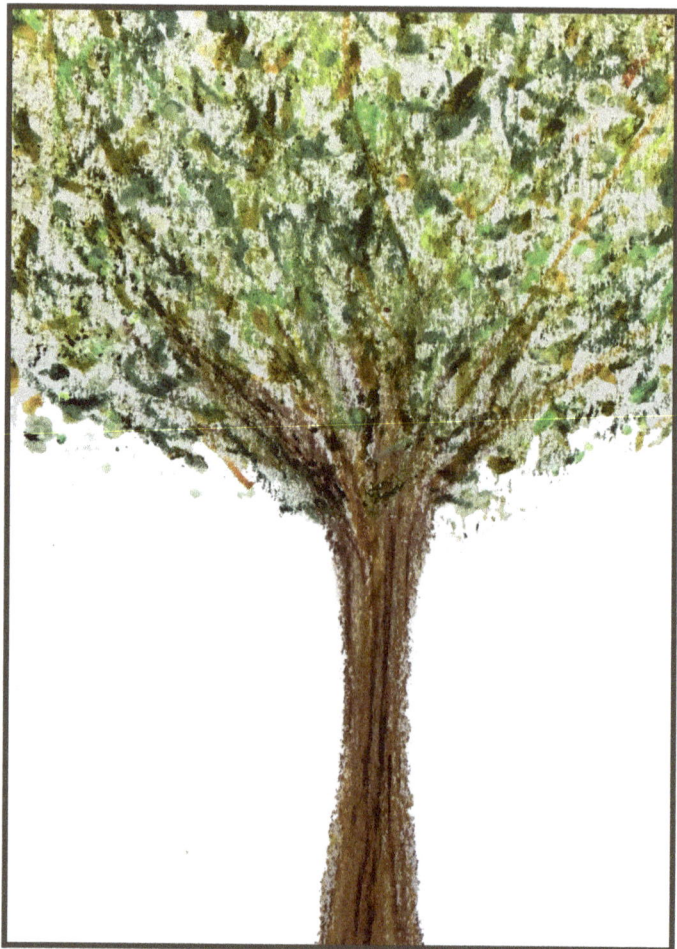

THE POET
ACKNOWLEDGING
OTHERS

I wish to acknowledge with gratitude:

1) The following print and online publications where several poems included in this collection were first published, during 2016-2019:

"Child In Me" in *Jeannie's Brave Childhood: Behavior and Healing through the Lens of Attachment and Trauma* by Janyne McConnaughey.

"Something Is Coming" (before current revision) in the story-in-verse picture book, *Something Is Coming To Our World: How a Backyard Bird Sees Christmas* by Catherine Lawton.

"Worthy to Receive Glory" and "Look at Me" at ALTARWORK.

"Look at Me" and "May-Day Baskets" at GODSPACE.

2) Friends and fellow poets who read and reviewed my first collection of poetry, *Remembering Softly* (2016), and who have given me encouragement as a poet: Mary Harwell Sayler, Gary Hassig, Elaine Wright Colvin, Alice Scott-Ferguson.

3) Marlene Bagnull for inviting me to teach a poetry workshop at the Colorado Christian Writers Conference.

4) All my readers and reviewers who seem to "get" what the poems are trying to say, and who no doubt make the verses better by finding in them some meanings of their own.

5) My Facebook friends and blog followers who read and respond to the poems I post.

6) Those who graciously and sagaciously read some or all of the poems in this volume, and gave me helpful feedback: poet, writer and former classmate, Jesse Baird; friend and poet, Troy Turner; and especially my literary and loving sister, Beverly Coons.

7) My husband, Larry, and our children and grandchildren, whose interest and love spur me on. To them I desire to leave a legacy of wonder, thought, and faith. Several of the grandchildren enjoy writing poetry themselves. One of those, Breanna Slike, I want to thank, especially, for her lovely, sensitive art pieces gracing the cover and pages of this book.

INTRODUCING
THE POET

Like many of her readers, Catherine (Cathy) Lawton has come a long way. One of her first poems was published nationally in a Sunday School take-home paper, "Junior Joys," when she was twelve. During adolescence she composed verses on themes of friendship, romance, nature, and a touch of humor, which helped her through the constant adjustments of life as a preacher's kid, altogether living in eight towns and attending seven schools. After college, marriage, and while mothering young children, she wrote articles and stories for publication; and her faith poems appeared in *Herald of Holiness, Standard, Prayer Works, Living Streams,* and others. In 2016, the first book of her collected poems was released: *Remembering Softly: A Life In Poems.* The present collection, *Glimpsing Glory,* features poems written from 2016 through 2019.

Cathy's other published books include *Face to Face : A Novel, Journeys to Mother Love,* and *Something Is Coming To Our World.* She has contributed to several compilations and blogs. She has worked as a musician, a substitute teacher, an editor, and a publisher.

Having lived all her life in Colorado and California, Cathy loves road trips with her husband, Larry, through the western states of America, holidays and outings to mountains and seashores with their two grown children and their spouses and all six grandchildren.

Cathy seeks to live a contemplative life while participating in community both near and far and in important discussions human beings are having these days. She desires to encourage beauty and well-being in the world as she cultivates gardens, friendships, and artful books.

Find her author presence online at:

Webpage: http://cladach.com/catherine-lawton/
Twitter: @cath_lawton
Amazon: https://www.amazon.com/Catherine-Lawton/e/B001K8YLA6
Goodreads: https://www.goodreads.com/cathlawton

www.ingramcontent.com/pod-product-compliance
Lightning Source LLC
Chambersburg PA
CBHW041922090426
42741CB00019B/3445